A CourseGuide for

Organic Outreach

Kevin Harney

ZONDERVAN
REFLECTIVE

ZONDERVAN REFLECTIVE

A CourseGuide for Organic Outreach
Copyright © 2020 by Zondervan

Requests for information should be addressed to:
Zondervan, *3900 Sparks Dr. SE, Grand Rapids, Michigan 49546*

ISBN 978-0-310-11102-3 (softcover)

Printed in the United States of America

CONTENTS

Introduction 5

1. The Law of Love 7

2. Becoming Grace Bearers 10

3. Embracing the Bible and Truth 14

4. The One-Degree Rule 18

5. Everyone Plays 22

6. The Unseen Work 26

7. The Wonder of Encounter 29

8. Incarnational Living 33

9. Try Something 37

10. The Work of the Holy Spirit 41

11. Engaging in Spiritual Conversations 45

12. Telling Your Story 49

13. Sharing Good News 53

Introduction

atologia, soteriology, and pulmonary posture. Boyer traces the top-
ics on the following pages. Complete for a completely thread, since
may be lorem. The intervention de parangeos? A Christos
did not happen. Boyer these deutero, a single party of Christel, an
by Th. mean some alias the Christology Vere Christian Corroborated, A
Christel (tent) Antifere, tentiled it term.

Welcome to the *A CourseGuide for Organic Outreach*. These guides were
created for formal and informal students alike who want to engage
deeper in biblical, theological, or ministry studies. We hope this guide
will provide an opportunity for you to grow not only in your under-
standing, but also in your faith.

How to Use This Guide

This guide is meant to be used in conjunction with the book *Organic
Outreach for Ordinary People*. After you have read each chapter in the
book, the materials in this guide will help you review and assess what
you have learned. Application-oriented questions are included as well.

Each CourseGuide has been individually designed to best equip
you in your studies, but in general, you can expect the following com-
ponents. Most CourseGuides begin every chapter with a "You Should
Know" section, which highlights key terminology, people, and facts
to remember. This section serves as a helpful summary for directing
your studies. Reflection questions, typically two to three per chapter,
prompt you to summarize key points you've learned. Discussion questions invite you to an even deeper level of engagement. Finally, most
chapters will end with a short quiz to test your retention. You can find
the answer key to each quiz at the bottom of the page following it.

For Further Study

CourseGuides accompany books and videos from some of the world's
top biblical and theological scholars. They may be used independently,
or in small groups or classrooms, offering quality instruction to equip

students for academic and ministry pursuits. If you would like to
engage in further study with Zondervan's CourseGuides, the full lineup
may be viewed online. After completing your studies with *A Course-
Guide for Organic Outreach*, we recommend moving on to *A CourseGuide
for Tactics: A Game Plan for Discussing Your Christian Convictions* and *A
CourseGuide for Apologetics at the Cross*.

CHAPTER 1

The Law of Love

You Should Know

- Matthew 22:37–40: "'Love the Lord your God with all your heart and with all your soul and with all your mind.' This is the first and greatest commandment. And the second is like it: 'Love your neighbor as yourself.' All the Law and the Prophets hang on these two commandments."

- John 3:16–17: "For God so loved the world that he gave his one and only Son, that whoever believes in him shall not perish but have eternal life. For God did not send his Son into the world to condemn the world, but to save the world through him."

- Romans 5:6–8: "You see, at just the right time, when we were still powerless, Christ died for the ungodly. Very rarely will anyone die for a righteous person, though for a good person someone might possibly dare to die. But God demonstrates his own love for us in this: While we were still sinners, Christ died for us."

- The greatest motivator for evangelism is love.

- The most important question to ask yourself with outreach is, Do I love this person?

- The fuel of evangelism is a love of God's glory and the joy of seeing lost people saved.

- The first and primary seeker is God.

- The Greatest Commandment: love the Lord your God with all your heart and with all your soul and with all your mind; love your neighbor as yourself

- Organic outreach: evangelism that flows from the heart of God

- Three principles of growing a heart of love: Pray that God will give us a heart like Jesus's heart; study the life of Jesus; notice and connect with people who are far from God

Essay Questions

Short

1. At the start of this course, what are your initial feelings about doing outreach? How might it look to live the kind of love-driven life that naturally draws people to Jesus?

2. God's love for broken and sinful people is one of the most amazing truths revealed in the Bible. How do you think God's love should drive your outreach?

3. What are your motives when it comes to outreach? How much of them are love-driven?

Long

1. Who is one spiritually disconnected person you know with whom you hope to share the gospel? How can you cultivate a deeper love for them in order to draw them closer to Jesus?

Quiz

1. (T/F) The starting point of effective outreach is a system, a program, and a specific presentation.

2. (T/F) Without a heart deeply in love with God and people, no outreach strategy will work.

3. What brought God from heaven to earth, moved Jesus to empty himself and take on human flesh, and allowed nails to be driven into the hands and feet of the perfect and pure son of God?

   a) Guilt
   b) Obligation
   c) Love
   d) Selfishness

4. (T/F) The God who came to seek and save the lost invites us into the same mission.

5. What should motivate us to do the work of evangelism and reach out to spiritually disconnected people?
    a) The desire to carve another notch on our spiritual belts
    b) A deep sense of guilt or fear
    c) The need to fill up the seats in our worship center
    d) Love for God and love for people.

6. Before anything else, what must organic outreach be?
    a) Program-driven
    b) Love-driven
    c) Money-driven
    d) Tactic-driven

7. What is the best and most effective driving force for evangelism?
    a) Church events
    b) Sincere love
    c) Gospel-sharing outlines
    d) Intellectual arguments.

8. What happens with our outreach as we respond to the loving mercy and amazing grace of God?
    a) Outreach becomes more complicated
    b) Outreach happens naturally
    c) We do outreach out of fear and guilt
    d) We rely on a specific presentation to do outreach

9. To begin growing a heart of love for those who are lost, broken, and wandering far from God, we can:
    a) Pray that God will give us a heart like Jesus's heart
    b) Study the life of Jesus
    c) Notice and connect with people who are far from God
    d) All of the above

10. (T/F) Evangelism, fueled by programs, presentations, and guilt, will become a natural and unstoppable force for reaching people for Christ.

ANSWER KEY

1. F, 2. T, 3. C, 4. T, 5. D, 6. B, 7. B, 8. B, 9. D, 10. F

CHAPTER 2

Becoming Grace Bearers

You Should Know

- Ephesians 2:8–9: "For it is by grace you have been saved, through faith — and this is not from yourselves, it is the gift of God — not by works, so that no one can boast."

- 2 Corinthians 5:21: "God made him who had no sin to be sin for us, so that in him we might become the righteousness of God."

- Justice is getting what we deserve.

- Mercy is not getting what we deserve.

- Grace is getting what we don't deserve.

- Our primary outreach message: the good news of God's grace offered in Jesus

- Two interlocking aspects of grace: the God we worship is the author of grace; we are sinners saved by grace

- Grace bearer: a Christian who lives each day with a profound awareness of God's love for them and infuses their life with the amazing grace of God for others

- Four marks of a grace bearer: reckless love, generous forgiveness, sacrificial sharing, and openness to others

- The label Jesus gladly wore: friend of tax collectors and "sinners"

Essay Questions

Short

1. If we don't personally get this whole grace thing, our organic outreach will suffer. So how are you doing at receiving God's offer of grace each day? What can you do to open your heart to receive God's grace more fully?

2. Grace bearers are marked by behaviors and attitudes that stand out in this graceless world: reckless love; generous forgiveness; sacrificial sharing; and an openness to different people. How are you doing in each of these areas?

3. Do you tend to avoid certain people or groups of people because you see them as "sinful" or a threat? What can you do to connect with someone who is different from you?

Long

1. Consider all the ways you've gotten what you don't deserve. How have you seen God's grace made evident in your life—in big ways and small ways?

Quiz

1. (T/F) If we are going to be effective in sharing the good news of Jesus, we must truly understand and receive the grace of God.

2. (T/F) We are quick to cry for justice when we have been wronged, and equally as swift to demand justice when we are the perpetrator.

3. What do we call it when we get what we don't deserve?

   a) Justice
   b) Mercy
   c) Grace
   d) Karma

4. God deals with the need for his own justice and we get what we don't deserve through:

    a) Animal sacrifices

    b) Our good works

    c) The work of Christ on the cross

    d) A cosmic get-out-of-jail-free card

5. Because Christ has been judged in our place, what don't we receive that we deserve?

    a) Heaven

    b) Punishment for our sins

    c) God's love

    d) A loving community

6. Organic outreach, motivated by love, must be infused with:

    a) Proven evangelistic programs

    b) Biblically accurate presentations

    c) The amazing grace of God

    d) Personal guilt and fear

7. We must always remember that our primary message in outreach is:

    a) The need for people to earn their salvation with good works

    b) The good news of God's grace offered in Jesus

    c) The bad news of hell

    d) None of the above

8. What are two distinct and interlocking aspects of grace?

    a) The God we worship is the author of grace

    b) We are sinners saved by grace

    c) We earn salvation by what we do

    d) Both A & B

    e) Both A & C

9. We deserved hell, but instead we have been given something we don't deserve:

    a) The love and friendship of God

    b) An eternal home with him in heaven

c) Neither A nor B
d) Both A & B

10. Which of the following behaviors and attitudes mark grace bearers?
a) Reckless love
b) Generous forgiveness
c) Sacrificial sharing
d) An open heart to different people
e) All of the above

CHAPTER 3

Embracing the Bible and Truth

You Should Know

- John 14:6–7: "Jesus answered, 'I am the way and the truth and the life. No one comes to the Father except through me. If you really know me, you will know my Father as well. From now on, you do know him and have seen him.'"

- Humble certainty is the humble submission of our lives to the teaching of Scripture with confident assurance that it is the very Word of God and our authority for life.

- The source of truth and sound doctrine is God's Word.

- Doctrine matters because what we believe determines how we live, love, and reach out to the world.

- The major factor that compels 9 out of 10 unchurched people to choose a church is doctrine.

- Biblical reality #1: God's passionate love is greater than we can comprehend and was revealed in the sacrifice of Jesus.

- Biblical reality #2: People are lost without Jesus.

- Biblical reality #3: Salvation is found in Jesus alone.

- Biblical reality #4: Heaven and hell are real, and real people will spend eternity in either place.

- Two streams of thought affecting people's view of heaven and hell: the hope of heaven is done away with a focus on making this life a better place; no problem with the idea of heaven, but uncomfortable with the biblical teaching on hell

Essay Questions

Short

1. The Church has always insisted upon what the Bible teaches with staggering clarity: salvation is found in Jesus, and only in him. How committed are you to this biblical truth when it comes to organic outreach?

2. How can you grow in your awareness that real people will spend eternity separated from God in hell if they refuse to accept the free gift of forgiveness that is found in Jesus Christ alone?

3. What has helped you to love and grow in your knowledge of the Bible? How can you continue to grow in your commitment to know and follow the truth revealed in Scripture?

Long

1. In what ways are Christians compromising their faith or questioning core beliefs that have been held by the church throughout its history? What do you think are some of the possible consequences of this trend to "question everything"?

Quiz

1. What is the source of truth and sound doctrine?
   a) My church's statement of faith
   b) God's Word
   c) Church tradition
   d) None of the above

2. (T/F) When we let the Word of God define our beliefs and form our doctrine, we naturally want to share the good news of God's love with others.

3. Upon what have the core, unifying beliefs of the Christian faith always been founded?

   a) Modern innovative and revolutionary thinking
   b) The Bible
   c) Church tradition
   d) A local church's statement of faith

4. Doctrine matters because what we believe determines:

   a) How we live
   b) How we love
   c) How we reach out to the world
   d) All of the above

5. (T/F) The sobering fact is our doctrine doesn't matter to those who are spiritual seekers; unchurched people don't care about what we believe.

6. When it comes to what we believe, Jesus taught us to have:

   a) Humble certainty
   b) Humble uncertainty
   c) A little of both
   d) Neither A nor B

7. If we take the Bible seriously, what sobering realities face us?

   a) The love of God revealed in the sacrifice of Jesus
   b) People are lost without Jesus
   c) Salvation is found in Jesus alone
   d) The reality of heaven and hell
   e) All of the above

8. (T/F) The word of God teaches that the bloody, horrible, sacrificial death of Jesus was necessary to pay for our sins.

9. The notion that all religions are equally valid and lead to salvation has:

   a) Ample biblical support
   b) Some biblical support

c) No biblical support
d) Enough biblical support

10. What does God want us to understand about people without Jesus?
   a) They are truly honored
   b) They are truly lucky
   c) They are truly all right
   d) They are truly lost

The One-Degree Rule

You Should Know

- Matthew 9:36–38: "When he saw the crowds, he had compassion on them, because they were harassed and helpless, like sheep without a shepherd. Then he said to his disciples, 'The harvest is plentiful but the workers are few. Ask the Lord of the harvest, therefore, to send out workers into his harvest field.'"

- The One-Degree Rule is a way to honestly assess where you are in your outreach by asking the question, "How can I raise my evangelistic temperature by one degree *today*?"

- The goal of the One-Degree Rule goal is to create an organic lifestyle of evangelism, in which we are always focused on growing in our passion for evangelism.

- Evangelistic temperature is the level of our evangelistic passion on a scale of 1 to 10.

- The existence of hell is a powerful motivator for sharing the gospel.

- Evangelistic temperature tactic #1: Engage in prayer consistently.

- Evangelistic temperature tactic #2: Make time to be with those who are far from God.

- Evangelistic temperature tactic #3: Tell stories about spiritual conversations with other believers.

- Evangelistic temperature tactic #4: Make time in your home, church, and workplace to celebrate whenever someone takes a step forward in faith.

- Evangelistic temperature tactic #5: Spend time reflecting on eternity and the eternal consequences facing those who don't know Jesus.

Essay Questions

Short

1. When Jesus looked upon the crowds the Gospels tell us he had compassion on them, because they were harassed and helpless. What is your heart-reaction when you consider those in your life who are far from God?

2. How much time do you spend in a normal week with people who are not yet followers of Jesus? How might it look to adjust your schedule to make more time to connect with people who are far from God?

3. The existence of heaven and hell is not the only reason we share the gospel, but it is a powerful motivator. Why is this the case? How do you think should reflecting on eternity raise your spiritual temperature?

Long

1. What is your evangelistic temperature in this season of your life? Take an honest assessment of where you're at. What can you do to raise your outreach temperature by one degree? What do you need to change, what do you need to do differently?

Quiz

1. What do we all have that gauges our level of enthusiasm for reaching out to people with the love of God?

   a) An evangelistic pulse
   b) An evangelistic temperature
   c) An evangelistic energy field
   d) An evangelistic responsibility

2. (T/F) It is our responsibility to keep our hearts burning hot and our lives engaged in reaching out.

3. (T/F) Usually the problem in the evangelistic equation is not with Christian workers who are called to reap the harvest, but with the world and those who are spiritually disconnected.

4. The One-Degree Rule:
   a) Acknowledges the reality that we need to increase our outreach temperature consistently
   b) Is a way to honestly assess where you are in your outreach temperature
   c) Asks the question, "How can I raise my evangelistic temperature by one degree *today*?"
   d) All of the above

5. (T/F) As our evangelistic temperature goes up, our effectiveness in outreach increases as well.

6. The point of the One-Degree Rule self-evaluation is:
   a) To compare ourselves with others to see how we measure up evangelistically
   b) To create an organic lifestyle in which we are always focused on growing in our passion for evangelism
   c) To make sure we fulfill our Christian duty
   d) To ensure we are winning as many souls for Christ as possible

7. (T/F) The biggest issue is not whether your evangelistic temperature is at a three, five, or eight, but that you can identify where you are.

8. The goal of using the One-Degree Rule is to honestly assess where you are and then ask the next question:
   a) "How can I raise my evangelistic skills by one degree today?"
   b) "How can I raise my evangelistic prospects by one degree today?"
   c) "How can I raise my evangelistic temperature by one degree today?"
   d) "How can I raise my evangelistic knowledge by one degree today?"

9. The best way to stoke the fire and raise your spiritual temperature for outreach is to:

    a) Engage in prayer for outreach consistently
    b) Make time to be with those who are far from God
    c) Tell stories about spiritual conversations and celebrate spiritual conversions
    d) Spend time reflecting on eternity and the eternal consequences of rejecting Jesus
    e) All of the above

10. How often should Christians do a self-assessment of their evangelistic temperature and take steps to increase it by one degree?

    a) Rarely
    b) Never
    c) Regularly
    d) Doesn't matter

CHAPTER 5

Everyone Plays

You Should Know

- Matthew 5:14–16: "You are the light of the world. A town built on a hill cannot be hidden. Neither do people light a lamp and put it under a bowl. Instead they put it on its stand, and it gives light to everyone in the house. In the same way, let your light shine before others, that they may see your good deeds and glorify your Father in heaven."

- God's plan for outreach is that every Christian gets off the sidelines and onto the field to play.

- Two realities addressed by Jesus's "You are the salt of the earth": salt makes people thirsty; salt preserves

- Two realities addressed by Jesus's "You are the light of the world": light allows us to walk confidently; light drives away fear

- Confrontational outreach: a biblical way of doing outreach that gently confronts people about their spiritual condition and relationship with God

- Intellectual outreach: a biblical way of doing outreach that focuses on using intellectual arguments and answering people's questions

- Interpersonal outreach: a biblical way of doing outreach that focuses on building relational bridges to people

- Testimonial outreach: a biblical way of doing outreach that focuses on telling stories of God's grace and power that draw people to the Savior

- Invitational outreach: a biblical way of doing outreach that focuses on connecting spiritual seekers to people and places where God's presence is evident

- Service outreach: a biblical way of doing outreach that focuses on serving faithfully through Spirit-anointed acts to open people up to God's love

Essay Questions

Short

1. Why do you think some people tend to sit on the bench when it comes to outreach? What might you do to help people you know get on the field and engage in this important calling?

2. Who is one Christian you have watched over the years who has modeled being salt and light in this world? What can you learn from this person's example?

3. What kind of outreach activity that you've engaged in has felt the most natural? What has felt the most forced and foreign to you?

Long

1. You might not have the gift of evangelism, but you *are* called to engage in the ministry of outreach. Are you convinced that God is calling you to engage in outreach in new and fresh ways? If not, what is standing in the way? If so, what's your next step? How might it look to deliberately reach out to people in your life by being salt and light?

Quiz

1. (T/F) Evangelism is not a spectator sport. God invites every follower of Jesus to get off the sidelines and onto the field of outreach.

2. (T/F) In the church, when everyone plays, we develop a healthy sense of individualism.

3. What do people who say "I can't do that!" discover about themselves when they commit to evangelism?

   a) God doesn't want to use them anyway
   b) God wants to use them, but in something other than evangelism
   c) They can do other things, just not evangelism
   d) God can use them to share his grace and his message of hope.

4. (T/F) As people engage in outreach and pray for their lost friends and neighbors, a passion for souls is ignited by God's Holy Spirit.

5. What is God's primary plan for spreading the message and the good news of his Son?

   a) The twelve apostles
   b) The early church fathers
   c) Every single Christian on the planet
   d) Seminary-trained pastors and teachers

6. Jesus said, "You are the salt of the earth." To what two spiritual realities does this analogy point?

   a) Salt makes people thirsty, and our passion for God should make people thirsty, too
   b) Salt preserves, and God wants us to be agents of preservation sprinkled throughout the world
   c) Neither A nor B
   d) Both A & B

7. Jesus also said, "You are the light of the world." To what two spiritual realities does this analogy point?

   a) Light allows us to walk confidently, so when people look at us they should see a confident trust because of the light of Christ
   b) Light drives away fear, so when believers walk in Jesus's light and shine as his light, the fears of this world flee
   c) Neither A nor B
   d) Both A & B

8. (T/F) There is only one way to do evangelism, so your own way of doing outreach should not grow organically out of who you are.

9. (T/F) The key to outreach is inviting the Spirit of God to direct you as you look for approaches that match your wiring and personality.

10. There are many different biblical models of doing outreach, including these approaches:

    a) Intellectual
    b) Testimonial
    c) Invitational
    d) Serving
    e) All of the above

CHAPTER 6

The Unseen Work

You Should Know

- Effective outreach cornerstone: prayer

- Prayer walking: the practice of moving consistently through an area and praying as the Holy Spirit leads

- Triple-Five prayers: an evangelistic prayer where you pray for five people for a minute apiece, five days a week

- Prayer for workers: praying for the Lord of the harvest to send workers into the harvest fields

- Scripture prayer: allowing the Word of God to shape our prayers

- Listening prayer: asking the Holy Spirit to shape our prayers for family and friends by taking time in silent waiting

- Fruit of the Spirit prayers: praying for specific fruits of the Spirit in Galatians 5:22–23 to grow in the lives of specific people

- Warfare prayers: fortifying ourselves as we engage the battle of outreach through prayer and praying against the work of the enemy

- Three words of counsel when praying against the devil's work: ask God for discernment to see where the enemy is at work; pray against the work of the devil in the name of Jesus; commit to praying with other believers

Essay Questions

Short

1. What steps can you take to engage more passionately in praying for those who are not yet in God's family?

2. Who do you know who models a life of committed and fervent prayer? What can you learn from this person's example and lifestyle?

3. Describe a kind of prayer that most naturally ignites your heart as you intercede for family members, neighbors, and friends who are unbelievers.

Long

1. Nothing we do as Christians is more dangerous than prayer. How seriously do you take prayer, especially when it comes to outreach? What are some obstacles that keep you from praying, and what can you do to remove them? Which of the various prayer ideas in this session seem most natural for you, and how might you incorporate them into your prayer life for effective outreach?

Quiz

1. What is the cornerstone of effective outreach?
   a) Intellectual arguments
   b) Prayer
   c) Church programs
   d) Evangelistic tactics

2. (T/F) We unleash heavenly power when we pray for lost people. We are also called to pray for ourselves and other believers to enter the harvest fields with God's good news.

3. (T/F) There are far more dangerous things Christians can do spiritually than pray.

4. Accomplishing the most from outreach comes from:
   a) Outreach brochures
   b) Step-by-step presentations
   c) Evangelistic events
   d) The power of prayer

5. (T/F) There are all sorts of creative ways to pray for people who are spiritually disconnected.

6. The issue is not finding "the right way to pray," but:

   a) Discovering appropriate ways to pray
   b) Discovering creative ways to pray
   c) Discovering timely ways to pray
   d) Discovering traditional ways to pray

7. At minimum, how often should you commit to doing prayer walks on your streets or in your neighborhood?

   a) Daily
   b) Weekly
   c) Monthly
   d) Yearly

8. What is an important component of doing Triple-Five prayers?

   a) Making a list of people who are far from God
   b) Praying for five people, a minute apiece, for five days a week
   c) Keeping a list of people who need prayer some place you will be reminded to pray on a regular basis
   d) All of the above

9. What is required for listening prayers?

   a) Active praying
   b) Time in silent waiting
   c) A group of people
   d) None of the above

10. What advice should we heed when we seek to pray against the work of the devil in this world and in the lives of those who are under his sway?

    a) Ask God for discernment to see where the enemy is at work
    b) Pray against the work of the devil in the name of Jesus
    c) Commit to praying with other believers
    d) All of the above

CHAPTER 7

The Wonder of Encounter

You Should Know

- 2 Chronicles 7:14: "If my people, who are called by my name, will humble themselves and pray and seek my face and turn from their wicked ways, then I will hear from heaven, and I will forgive their sin and will heal their land."

- Numbers 6:24–26: "The Lord bless you and keep you; the Lord make his face shine on you and be gracious to you; the Lord turn his face toward you and give you peace."

- Seven suggestions for praying with people: keep it brief; use common language; extend a hand if appropriate; pray for specific things; pray in Jesus's name; check in with their life; be sensitive to the situation

- Jail Prayer: showing genuine seriousness and care by praying over prisoners

- Bless Me: extending our hand and placing it on someone to speak a prayer of blessing, such as Numbers 6:24–26

- Family Prayer: praying with family members who are hurting over some decision, situation, or need

- Restaurant Prayers: asking our servers in restaurants if they have any needs you can pray about

- A Prayer of Openness: "God, I don't know if you are real, but if you are out there, please show yourself to me."

- A Prayer for Love-Revelation: "If you are out there, God, and you love me, will you help me feel your love?"

- A Prayer for Need-Meeting: "If you are real and as powerful as people say, could you answer my prayers and meet my needs?"

Essay Questions

Short

1. What might keep you from asking your unbelieving friends, "May I pray with you?" Are these obstacles enough to keep you from trying?

2. What do you think might happen if your non-Christian friends allowed you to pray with them? How might your relationship with them grow if they began to freely share needs and joys with you and you began to consistently lift them up in prayer?

3. Of the pictures of praying with people and organic prayer examples offered in this session, which do you most resonate with? Which do you think would be most effective for those you know?

Long

1. Who are two or three non-Christians God has placed in your life? What are some of their needs today? What are their joys? How do you think they'd respond if they shared a struggle and you said, "Would you mind if I took a moment to pray with you?"

Quiz

1. What is an opportunity for God to show up and reveal his power with unbelievers?

    a) Eating with them
    b) Preaching at them
    c) Praying with them
    d) Singing to them

2. (T/F) Organic outreach is propelled forward when we learn to pray with those who are not yet part of God's family.

3. (T/F) Most people will not gratefully receive prayer when you offer it.

4. What should you keep in mind when you pray with people?
   a) Make your prayers long
   b) Use religious language
   c) Pray for a person's specific needs or joys
   d) Pray in the name of the god with whom they're comfortable

5. (T/F) When you're praying, it is okay to extend a hand if it's appropriate, because there is power in touch.

6. What will happen once people realize you are serious about lifting them and their needs up in prayer?
   a) They will turn and go the other way
   b) They will begin to seek you out and ask for prayer
   c) They will resent your relationship
   d) None of the above

7. What kind of prayer offers Numbers 6:24–26 as a prayer?
   a) Jail Prayer
   b) Bless Me Prayer
   c) Family Prayer
   d) Restaurant Prayer

8. What kind of prayer is geared toward asking your server if they have any needs you can lift up in prayer?
   a) Jail Prayer
   b) Bless Me Prayer
   c) Family Prayer
   d) Restaurant Prayer

9. What can happen when you pray with an unbeliever?
   a) God's presence can be felt as he draws near in the power of the Spirit

b) Spiritual seekers can see that your faith is real and you have a relationship with God
c) Doors are opened for ongoing spiritual conversations as they ask you questions
d) All of the above

10. What kind of prayer will help people know that God has affection for them?

a) A prayer of love
b) A prayer of openness
c) A prayer of invitation
d) A prayer of need

CHAPTER 8

Incarnational Living

You Should Know

- Close proximity is the commitment to keeping our lives intersecting with people who are spiritual seekers.

- Incarnation is a theological term that describes God's coming into human history.

- Cultural voyeurism is the temptation to gaze on the things of this world to satisfy a sinful desire.

- Incarnational living: reflecting Jesus's love, showing his heart, and incarnating his presence wherever God sends us as his ambassadors on this earth

- Incarnational living step 1: engage the cultural landscape by jumping into your community with enthusiasm

- Incarnational living step 2: learn to listen as Jesus listened to people

- Incarnational living step 3: make space for people who are broken, lonely, hurting, and outcast

- Incarnational living step 4: live sacrificially by choosing to serve those in need, sacrifice where we can, and suffer for the sake of the gospel out of love for people

- Incarnational living step 5: overflow with joy, which should blow away the world

Essay Questions

Short

1. Describe your *close proximity*. How are you at keeping your life intersecting with people who are spiritual seekers? How can you make more time and space to develop new relationships with non-believers and bring Jesus's presence into your world?

2. What do you think about the two warnings given in this session when it comes to engaging and connecting in our culture? Which one are you most susceptible to?

3. Do you consider yourself a good listener? Or are you quick to interrupt people and point out what's wrong? How might it look to follow Jesus by cultivating a habit of listening and relating to people right where they are?

Long

1. This session explores a number of steps and aspects of incarnational living. Which do you find you already engage in naturally? In which do you feel you could use some growth? Make a plan for focusing on incarnational living in order to reach out to those around you.

Quiz

1. People need to hear about Jesus. They also need to:
   a) Get him
   b) See him
   c) Touch him
   d) Hear him

2. (T/F) Incarnational outreach, relational evangelism, and organic outreach are similar names for the same idea.

3. (T/F) Incarnational ministry reflects the light, love, and presence of Christ wherever we go by seeking to be like Jesus and to bring his presence into each situation we enter.

4. There are five steps to incarnational living, what are they?

   a) Engage the cultural landscape; learn to listen; make space for people; live for yourself; overflow with joy
   b) Avoid the cultural landscape; learn to listen; make space for people; live sacrificially; overflow with joy
   c) Engage the cultural landscape; learn to listen; make space for people; live sacrificially; overflow with joy
   d) Engage the cultural landscape; learn to talk; make space for people; live sacrificially; overflow with joy

5. What are two words of warning when we engage the cultural landscape?

   a) Be aware of the temptation to engage in cultural voyeurism; make sure you are influencing people and the culture with the truth of the gospel and not the other way around
   b) Be aware of the temptation to engage in cultural avoidance; make sure you are influencing people and the culture with the truth of the gospel and not the other way around
   c) Be aware of the temptation to engage in cultural voyeurism; make sure the people and culture are influencing you and not the other way around
   d) None of the above

6. *Cultural voyeurism* can include:

   a) Watching movies and television
   b) Visiting websites
   c) Hanging out in bars or places on the fringe of society
   d) All of the above

7. (T/F) Relational evangelism begins with speaking, rather than listening.

8. What are some ways Jesus made space for people?

   a) He stopped and blessed
   b) He opened blind eyes
   c) He restored the sick and the suffering
   d) All of the above

9. If we are going to bring the presence and Spirit of Jesus to this world, we must:

a) Preach the gospel daily to those who are broken, lonely, and outcast

b) Make space daily for those who are broken, lonely, and outcast

c) Bring to church weekly those who are broken, lonely, and outcast

d) Memorize evangelistic techniques regularly to share with those who are broken, lonely, and outcast

10. What are the good things God gives Christians that give them reason to overflow with joy?

a) Our sins are washed away

b) We are secure in God's hands

c) We are given gifts of the Spirit

d) All of the above

Try Something

You Should Know

- Matthew 9:10: "While Jesus was having dinner at Matthew's house, many tax collectors and sinners came and ate with him and his disciples."

- "Come walk with me" is an invitation to people you know to join you in the regular activities of your life.

- Serving others shows the world that Jesus is alive and active in the world through acts of service; it's a way to model Jesus's love and compassion.

- Our part in bringing life-change to people is to spread the seed of the gospel liberally.

- Matthew Parties: a time for followers of Jesus to let their different worlds — church and non-church worlds — intersect and see what happens

- Learning together: a way to connect with nonbelievers who tend to think their way through life instead of feeling their way around issues

- Providing Christian resources: a way to help people who need more space to work through things on their own to explore the Christian faith

- Church-based gathering invites: looking at the events and programs your church offers, identifying something that happens at your church that looks like a natural fit for an unchurched friend, then saying a prayer and inviting them

- Thirty-Second Rule: a commitment to pause at specific times in the flow of the day to recalibrate our hearts and eyes toward the people around us by allowing the Holy Spirit to tune us in to *what* he would have us to do and *who* he would have us love

- Three Thirty-Second Rule questions: What would the Spirit of God prompt me to pray as I walk into this portion of my day? Who does God want me to notice right now? How might I extend the love of God and grace of Jesus in this situation?

Essay Questions

Short

1. Some people have established a specific evangelistic program or series of steps they believe a Christian can use with all people in all situations. What are some potential pitfalls of this approach to outreach?

2. Recall the story about Henry in the introduction to this session. This story presents some unconventional approaches to outreach. How has God opened doors for you to connect with non-believers through unique and surprising ways?

3. In your efforts to scatter the seed of the gospel, what is one approach that just did not work for you? Why wasn't this approach a good fit? What is one way you have reached out that clicked and felt natural? Why do you think this approach fits you?

Long

1. This session reminds us that our part is not to transform hearts; it's to spread the seed of the gospel liberally. Where do you work and live, and who do you know that you can throw some seed out there, try something new, and see what God does?

Quiz

1. (T/F) There is only one gospel, and there is only one way to express it and to reach people who are spiritually disconnected.

2. (T/F) Sharing God's love doesn't always come with clear instructions. Sometimes we just need to press on and try different things as we interact with people who are not yet followers of Jesus.

3. (T/F) We should wait to scatter seed when the soil looks rich, the conditions are perfect, and success is guaranteed.

4. When you reach out to someone you should:
    a) Have a plan and execute it
    b) Bring them to an evangelistic program
    c) Know a three-step approach to evangelistic success and use it
    d) Seek the wisdom of the Spirit, pray for God's grace, and try something

5. What is our job when it comes to doing outreach?
    a) Guarantee gospel results
    b) Scatter gospel seed and water it
    c) Successfully execute a gospel-sharing technique
    d) All of the above

6. When we face obstacles to sharing the gospel we should:
    a) Be alarmed, because obstacles aren't common
    b) Don't be alarmed, because obstacles are common
    c) Pray harder
    d) Share the gospel harder

7. What should you invite your unbelieving friends to join you in doing when you ask them to "Come walk with me"?
    a) Primarily church programs
    b) Overtly faith-based activities
    c) Regular activities of life
    d) Evangelistic events

8. Matthew Parties encourage followers of Jesus:
    a) To keep their "church friends" and "other friends" from intersecting
    b) To let their "church friends" and "other friends" intersect

c) To compartmentalize their lives
d) None of the above

9. When is it okay to invite people to a church service, event, or program?

a) The first time you meet someone
b) When an evangelist comes to town
c) When something that's happening looks like a natural fit
d) It's never okay

10. When it comes to the Thirty-Second Rule, we are encouraged to:

a) Pray
b) Notice
c) Take action
d) All of the above

CHAPTER 10

The Work of the Holy Spirit

You Should Know

- Acts 1:8: "But you will receive power when the Holy Spirit comes on you; and you will be my witnesses in Jerusalem, and in all Judea and Samaria, and to the ends of the earth."

- 1 Corinthians 3:7: "Neither the one who plants nor the one who waters is anything, but only God, who makes things grow."

- An essential element of sharing our faith: learning to listen for God's leading as we work in partnership with the Holy Spirit

- Our gospel work is to clearly and faithfully communicate the message of the gospel.

- The one who convicts sinners of their need for the grace of Jesus is the Spirit of God.

- What if I lack the power to reach out effectively? The Bible presupposes that we lack the strength, power, and boldness to reach out effectively. We find our strength and passion as we tune into the presence and voice of the Holy Spirit.

- What if I don't know what to do next? Reliance on the Holy Spirit is essential. We can be confident that God is ready to guide us as we reach out to others.

- What if I come under the enemy's attack? Recognize his attack, cry out for the power of the Spirit to overcome the enemy, and draw near to God.

- The two parties involved in saving people: we do our part by spreading gospel-seed; only God saves people

- Two things we don't get regarding someone's spiritual journey: *credit* when someone comes to faith in Jesus; *blame* if someone remains hard-hearted

Essay Questions

Short

1. Read the quote by Bill Hybels on the first page of this session's chapter. How might it look in your life to be "cooperative with the Holy Spirit" and have "an ear fine-tuned to the promptings of the Holy Spirit"? How would this impact your outreach?

2. Henry's story is a reminder that the Holy Spirit is at work in the conversion process. Describe a time you saw the Spirit intervene and do something no person could have done in the process of leading someone to Jesus.

3. Are there ways you subtly seek to take credit for the work God does in reaching people and changing lives? Are there ways you take too much responsibility for people's response to Jesus? What do you think might be the potential dangers of each?

4. How have you seen the Holy Spirit move hearts and touch lives? As you reflect on the work of the Spirit in the past, how might you be inspired to trust in the Spirit's work in the future?

Long

1. Of the three most common questions people often wrestle with when they partner with God in the work of outreach, which do you find yourself asking? Why is that? How might it look to trust the Spirit to help?

Quiz

1. (T/F) God can do his part, but only we can draw people to Jesus and change their lives.

2. What is one essential element to sharing our faith?

    a) Learning to listen for God's leading as we work in partnership with the Holy Spirit
    b) Learning the right evangelism techniques as we work in partnership with the Holy Spirit
    c) Learning how to use intellectual arguments as we work in partnership with the Holy Spirit
    d) Learning how to develop relationships as we work in partnership with the Holy Spirit

3. (T/F) The work of salvation belongs to God alone as he moves in our lives by the Holy Spirit. We can do our part, but only God saves people.

4. When someone comes to faith in Jesus:

    a) We get partial credit
    b) We get all the credit
    c) We get none of the credit
    d) We get equal credit with Jesus

5. When someone remains hard-hearted and doesn't come to faith in Jesus:

    a) We have to live with the blame
    b) We don't have to live with the blame
    c) We have to live with partial blame
    d) We have to share the blame with Jesus

6. What kind of partnership did Jesus say is essential to outreach?

    a) Partnership with evangelism programs
    b) Partnership with churches
    c) Partnership with the Spirit
    d) Partnership with people

7. How is a person convicted of sin?

    a) Through intellectual arguments
    b) At evangelistic events
    c) Because of outreach techniques
    d) By the Spirit

8. What if the we lack the power to reach out effectively?

   a) No problem! Just use a different evangelistic technique to reach out effectively.
   b) It's okay! The Bible presupposes we lack the power to reach out effectively.
   c) It's all right! Try harder at building the relationship to reach out effectively.
   d) All of the above

9. What if we don't know what to do next when we reach out?

   a) Do more research, then come back to the conversation.
   b) Bring your prospect to an evangelistic event, then trust the evangelist will do his job.
   c) Reliance on the Holy Spirit is essential; we don't have to figure it out on our own.
   d) Try a different outreach technique, then spend time figuring it out on your own.

10. What if we come under the enemy's attack?

   a) Recognize his attack, cry out for the power of the Spirit to overcome the enemy, and draw near to God.
   b) Recognize his attack, review your evangelistic presentation, and bring someone else along when you do outreach.
   c) Recognize his attack, research more intellectual arguments, and try harder.
   d) Don't worry, the enemy won't attack you if you engage in outreach.

ANSWER KEY

1. F, 2. A, 3. T, 4. C, 5. B, 6. C, 7. D, 8. B, 9. C, 10. A

CHAPTER 11

Engaging in Spiritual Conversations

You Should Know

- Spiritual conversations are a natural part of our lives where we let our faith overflow into our daily interactions and ordinary conversations in organic ways.

- Spiritual conversation: question about good things-What are some joys you are experiencing in this season of your life?

- Spiritual conversation: question about hurts and pains-What challenges and struggles are you facing?

- Spiritual conversation: question about faith-life-What is your personal history when it comes to faith and God?

- Spiritual conversation: question about personal beliefs-What do you believe about God?

- Spiritual conversation: question about perception of Christians-What is your perception of Christianity or of the Christian church?

- Truck-Sized Opening #1: "What did you do this weekend?"-Share about gathering with God's people for worship.

- Truck-Sized Opening #2: Sharing a struggle in your life-Give testimony to how God has shown up, sustained you, and helped you through.

- Truck-Sized Opening #3: Experiencing a time of blessing-Acknowledge that the good things you are experiencing come from the hand of a loving God.

- Truck-Sized Opening #4: Viewing beautiful creation-Don't be shy about acknowledging the one who made the heavens and the earth and everything in them.

Essay Questions

Short

1. What helps you enter naturally into spiritual conversations with family members and friends who are not yet followers of Jesus?

2. What pain and struggles have you faced in your life, and how has God been near you through these hard times? How might your story of God's comforting presence and sustaining power bring hope to others?

3. Do you agree that you should be willing to admit that you don't have all the answers and still struggle with some of your own questions when it comes to faith and the Bible? Why or why not?

Long

1. Using one of the scales discussed in this chapter (Engel and Norton's or Thom Rainer's), where would you place one or two of your non-believing friends? What level of spiritual conversation would be appropriate with each person? How might you help nudge the conversation to a new level of spiritual engagement?

Quiz

1. Spiritual conversations don't have to be:
   a) Natural and easy
   b) Forced and uncomfortable
   c) Fruitful and comfortable
   d) All of the above

2. (T/F) God wants our faith to overflow into our daily interactions in organic ways. If our faith is real, it will be part of our ordinary conversations.

3. Most people are open to entering a spiritual conversation, if we speak:

   a) With gentleness and respect
   b) With force and arguments
   c) With a plan and an outline
   d) All of the above

4. Spiritual conversations include:

   a) Sharing our testimony
   b) Presenting the gospel
   c) Sharing our pain and brokenness
   d) Sharing our questions about faith
   e) All of the above

5. (T/F) When we engage in spiritual conversations, we should appear as if we have it all together.

6. Seekers will never listen to us if we present ourselves as:

   a) Having the same kinds of problems that they have
   b) Perfect people, untouched by the pain and brokenness of the world
   c) Not having the answers to their important questions
   d) None of the above

7. When it comes to the Bible, as Christians it is important to have:

   a) A humble confidence
   b) An uncertain confidence
   c) Confident answers
   d) Uncertain answers

8. A clear biblical example of admitting we don't have all the answers is the blind man in John 9, because he:

   a) Was certain about what he knew and hid what he didn't know
   b) Was dishonest about his uncertainty and unconfident about what he knew
   c) Admitted what he did not know and affirmed what he did know
   d) None of the above

9. (T/F) Admitting we don't have all the answers will often open the door for ongoing conversation.

10. When we are in a spiritual conversation and someone asks a question we can't answer, it is usually wise:

   a) To make up an answer on the spot
   b) To say, "Let me do a little study or reflect on that and get back to you."
   c) To say, "That's a great question. Here's what I think."
   d) To say, "If you'd put that question in abeyance and ask me again when I'm finished making my point, I'll be sure to give you an answer."

CHAPTER 12

Telling Your Story

You Should Know

- Testimonies are the many stories of God's power and presence in our lives.

- Testimony reminder #1: Ask permission, don't be pushy-When you share, ask, "Would you mind if I told you a little about a way God has changed my life?"

- Testimony reminder #2: Use ordinary language-We can't assume nonbelievers will know what we mean when we refer to any number of Christian words when we share our story of faith.

- Testimony reminder #3: Start briefly, share more when appropriate-A short testimony is almost always better than a long one.

- Testimony reminder #4: Highlight God's presence and power-People want to know if this God you say is real has power to move in this world. If you have seen his power, tell the story.

- Testimony reminder #5: Clearly present the before-and-after-It helps people see the difference Jesus can make in a life; let the transforming work of God become the focus of a testimony.

- Testimony reminder #6: Share the source of life transformation-It is critical that we articulate that Jesus is the source of our life-change.

- Testimony reminder #7: Let joy shine through-Joy is a universal language. Knowing the Father, walking with Jesus, and being filled with the Holy Spirit should bring a flow of joy that is visible and contagious.

- Testimony reminder #8: Communicate with humility-A testimony is a humble declaration that God is moving in our lives and that we are grateful for what he is doing.

- Testimony reminder #9: You have many testimonies-When you share a testimony, make sure it's relevant for them.

Essay Questions

Short

1. What are some ways God is revealing his power and presence in your life right now? How can these experiences become testimonies in the months to come in order to reach out to someone you know?

2. How do you think a clearly presented testimony could impact a person you know who is not yet a follower of Jesus? How might you begin using more testimonies as you interact with spiritual seekers?

3. Take one of the examples from the previous question and expand it into a testimony, keeping in mind the nine helpful reminders from this session. It doesn't have to be long or miraculous—just a story that testifies to God's goodness and grace! (If you need direction, re-read the example stories at the start of this session's chapter.)

Long

1. Remember: Christians don't have just one testimony; we have many. In a sentence or two, list three examples of God's power and presence in your life, whether recently or in the past.

Quiz

1. (T/F) Christians don't have just one testimony; we have many.

2. (T/F) Sharing our testimony is the same thing as sharing God's story, the gospel.

3. (T/F) Many spiritually disconnected people don't believe we believe what we say we believe.

4. Our testimonies are:
   a) The things we've done to make us right with God
   b) Stories of God's power and presence in our lives
   c) What we believe about the gospel
   d) All of the above

5. When we give an authentic and passionate testimony, what do we declare?
   a) We have earned God's favor by what we have done
   b) God wants to bless us with prosperity
   c) We believe in a God who is active and powerful
   d) None of the above

6. A well-expressed testimony will communicate to your nonbelieving friends and family members that God is the one who can:
   a) Restore shattered hearts
   b) Set us free from fear and worry
   c) Wash away sin and remove the cloud of guilt
   d) Give new purpose and direction in life
   e) All of the above

7. When people hear stories of how God is moving and working in your life, they are faced with a profound reality:
   a) You really trust in what you do to make yourself right with God
   b) You really believe what you say you believe
   c) You really trust in God's prosperity
   d) You really practice what you preach

8. How should you respond when you are experiencing a time of blessing, joy, or celebration?
   a) Don't acknowledge the good things you are experiencing so that you don't offend someone.
   b) Acknowledge that the good things you are experiencing come from the hand of a loving God.

---

c) Acknowledge that the good things you are experiencing come from what you have done.

d) Acknowledge that the good things you are experiencing are because you've been chosen by God.

9. As you tell your story of God's movement and work in your life:

a) Make sure your blessing is central.

b) Make sure a gospel presentation is central.

c) Make sure your story is central.

d) Make sure God is central.

10. What helps people see the difference Jesus makes in our lives?

a) The good works of our life

b) The before-and-after picture of our life

c) The beliefs of our faith

d) The evangelistic events of our church

CHAPTER 13

Sharing Good News

You Should Know

- *Gospel* literally means "good news," since it is the message of hope speaking to the human condition of sin and promising forgiveness, purpose, and eternal life to those who believe.

- The Romans Road presentation: a step-by-step look at some key passages from the book of Romans that present core truths of the faith, including Romans 3:23, 6:23, 10:9–10, 10:13, 8:1, 12:1–2

- Do versus Done presentation: Being religious is spelled DO, and being a Christian is spelled DONE. For most people religion is what they *do*. Christianity is all about what God has *done*

- Romans 1:16–17: "For I am not ashamed of the gospel, because it is the power of God that brings salvation to everyone who believes: first to the Jew, then to the Gentile. For in the gospel the righteousness of God is revealed—a righteousness that is by faith from first to last, just as it is written: 'The righteous will live by faith.'"

- 1 Corinthians 15:3–5: "For what I received I passed on to you as of first importance: that Christ died for our sins according to the Scriptures, that he was buried, that he was raised on the third day according to the Scriptures, and that he appeared to Cephas, and then to the Twelve."

- Acts 4:12: "Salvation is found in no one else, for there is no other name under heaven given to mankind by which we must be saved."

- 1 Timothy 2:5–6: "For there is one God and one mediator between God and mankind, the man Christ Jesus, who gave himself as a ransom for all people. This has now been witnessed to at the proper time."

- Psalm 86:15: "But you, Lord, are a compassionate and gracious God, slow to anger, abounding in love and faithfulness."

- Romans 6:23: "For the wages of sin is death, but the gift of God is eternal life in Christ Jesus our Lord."

- 1 John 4:10: "This is love: not that we loved God, but that he loved us and sent his Son as an atoning sacrifice for our sins."

- 1 John 1:9: "If we confess our sins, he is faithful and just to forgive us our sins and purify us from all unrighteousness."

- Romans 10:9: "If you declare with your mouth, 'Jesus is Lord,' and believe in your heart that God raised him from the dead, you will be saved."

Essay Questions

Short

1. "Preach the gospel at all times. Use words when necessary." Do you agree with this statement? Why or why not?

2. Which of the presentations in this session would feel most natural if you had an opportunity to share the gospel with a specific person in your life?

3. Describe a time when you shared the gospel using one of the outreach approaches in this session. Now tell about a time you shared the message of Jesus using another presentation. What were those experiences like? What happened?

Long

1. We can love people, pray for them, and serve them, but there comes a time when they need to hear the message of Jesus Christ, the gospel. What is the gospel? Why do you think this might be true, that at some point people need to hear the gospel? Briefly explain how you would communicate the gospel.

Quiz

1. We can love people, pray for them, and serve them, but there comes a time when they need:

    a) To see your good works
    b) To hear the message of Jesus Christ, the gospel
    c) To hear your testimony
    d) To see how much God has blessed you

2. (T/F) Saving faith is found in Jesus alone.

3. Through what has God revealed truth to humanity?

    a) Scripture
    b) Jesus
    c) Our good works
    d) Both A & B

4. (T/F) We can present the message of Jesus in many ways, but the basic content of that message remains the same.

5. What does the Bible teach over and over again?

    a) That God helps those who help themselves
    b) That God requires people to work to earn his favor
    c) That God loves people more than words can express
    d) All of the above

6. How have human beings broken their relationship with God?

    a) By failing to live up to our personal best
    b) By following bad examples
    c) By sinning against God
    d) By polluting the world

7. The Bible teaches that God loves people more than words can express. How did he express this love? What is his greatest news ever?

    a) He solved our human problem by coming to this earth as a man and showed us a better example to follow.
    b) He solved our human problem by coming to this earth as a man and paying the price for our sins.

c) He solved our human problem by teaching us how to live up to our personal best.

d) He solved our human problem by teaching us a set of religious laws and rituals to follow.

8. How do we accept Jesus, have our sins washed away, and enter into a restored relationship with God?

a) By following Jesus's moral example
b) By performing God's religious laws and rituals
c) By living up to our personal best
d) By placing our faith in Jesus

9. What are the ABC's of salvation?

a) Accept; Believe; Convince
b) Accept; Behave; Confess
c) Accept; Believe; Confess
d) Apply; Believe; Confess

10. There is a need to clearly communicate the content of the gospel. What is there also a time to do?

a) Ask people if they are ready to cross the line of faith and accept Christ as their Lord and Savior
b) Ask people if they are ready to follow Jesus's example as a good moral teacher
c) Ask people if they are ready to fulfill the religious laws and rituals of Christianity
d) Ask people if they are ready to work to become right with God

Notes

www.ingramcontent.com/pod-product-compliance
Lightning Source LLC
Chambersburg PA
CBHW010921040426
42445CB00017B/1942